# 12 Tennis Secrets to Win More

## "What you should be doing and working on to win all the time!"

### By Joseph Correa

## COPYRIGHT PAGE

© 2013 12 Tennis Secrets to Win More!
ISBN 978-1-941525-10-4
All rights reserved. This book or any portion thereof may not be reproduced or used in any manner without the express written permission of the publisher except for brief book quotations for reviews on the book.

Scanning, uploading, and distributing of this book via the Internet or via any other means without the express permission of the publisher and author is illegal and punishable by law.

Only purchase authorized editions of this book. Please consult with your physician before training and using this book.
You can visit the author's website at tennisvideostore.com

## ABOUT THE AUTHOR

Hello, my name is Joseph Correa and I have been training and teaching tennis for over 15 years. I played professional tennis for years and am now a USPTR professional certified coach.

After years of competing and training with some of the best in the world I have learned that most people can be very successful in competition with the right mental, physical, and emotional training.

Proven scientific techniques, drills, and step by step phases must be performed to reach your peak and for that reason I have prepared the first group of training DVD's and books showing you how to reach your goals.

Through my work and teaching aids, I have helped hundreds of amateur and professional tennis players advance with their physical, mental, and performance goals to achieve great results.

I teach you everything I know you will need to reach your goals and hope you will enjoy and share these lessons and ideas with loved ones. To learn more about the different lessons taught through my books and DVD's go to www.tennisvideostore.com. Many more books will be coming out this year with some advanced drills and techniques.

Best of luck,

Joseph

## TABLE OF CONTENTS

COPYRIGHT PAGE
ABOUT THE AUTHOR

Tip #1: Toss the ball higher on your serve

Tip #2: Split step before every shot

Tip #3: Invest more time on your point of contact

Tip #4: Follow through on all your ground strokes

Tip #5: Work on serve consistency to win more often

Tip #6: Return more serves with better footwork

Tip #7: Warm up well before the match starts to begin successfully

Tip #8: Stretch after every match to be ready for your next opponent

Tip #9: Work every point of the match, especially the first points of very game

Tip #10: Close out matches decisively before it's too late

Tip #11: Stay positive no matter what the score or situation of the match

Tip #12: Use your brain to win more matches and develop your mental toughness

The best strategy book around: 32 Tennis Strategies for Today's Game

Bonus: 5 mistakes you probably don't know you're making
15 Bonus Serve Drills to Master Consistency, Spin, and Power

Would you do me a favor?

Other titles by Joseph Correa

# Tip #1: Toss the ball higher on your serve

Most people blame their hitting arm for their mistakes but the majority of the time it has nothing to do with your swinging arm. It's all about the tossing arm.

**The key elements for a good toss are:**

- Keep your tossing arm relaxed and make sure you hold the ball gently. You should be holding the ball with your finger tips and not with the palm of your hand.

- Work on placing the ball in the air instead of tossing the ball in the air. This will make your toss more precise and consistent.

- The best place to toss the ball is always about a foot out in front of your right shoulder if you were facing the court and serving a slice or flat serve. If you are serving a kick serve you should be tossing the ball behind your head or above your head, depending on how much arc you create with your back.
You should practice your toss at least 30 times before hitting an actual ball and at least 3 times per week.

If you have a bad toss you will never have a good serve so start paying more attention to your tossing arm if you want to improve your serve.

# Tip #2: Split step before every shot

Some people think their slowness requires more sprints or 5 miles runs but they don't know it's more about training smarter and not harder.

The "split step" is nothing more than a hop with both feet to help you prepare for your opponent's shot. Make sure they remain about at shoulder's distance apart to help you stay low.

The "split step" can be done with a low and quick hop or a high and slow hop depending on how fast the point is going. Go fast and short for quick rallies and points. Slow and high for high bouncing topspin shots and longer, slower rallies.

**When should you be doing the "split step"?**
Well there's a precise moment when you should do the hop. You should split step right when your opponent is making contact with the ball as to react the quickest to any direction that may be required of you.

**How do practice the split step?**
Jumping rope with both feet at the same time helps build strength and stamina so that you don't get tired of doing it during your match.

You can also stand at the base line and practice hopping back and forth with both feet at the same time while keeping your feet about shoulder distance apart.

Doing plyometric or jump training is very effective as well to help you improve your split step and over all jumping ability. The important thing here is to do the training over a soft surface and not overdo it or your knees will pay the price.

# Tip #3: Invest more time on your point of contact

# 12 Tennis Secrets to Win More!

Everyone thinks they're looking at the ball, and they are, but not the way it should be done to make clean contact.

Do you ever take the time to notice that all the posters of tennis pros always show them watching the ball when they make contact?

Well, that's because they know just how important it is to them and their game.

The secret is in learning to invest more time and keep your eyes on the ball at the point of contact and not look away too quickly at its destination. Once you've hit the ball there's nothing you can do to make it steer down into the court. All that matters is the moment you make contact.

**Try these techniques to help you invest more time in your point of contact:**

- when making contact with the ball try to see what number the ball has on it. It sounds crazy but don't think it's impossible. You can search for markings on the ball as well but trying to see what number is on the ball is enough of a challenge.

- try watching your racquet's shadow as you swing when you make contact to determine if your racquet is angled correctly as to make the ball go in the right direction. For some people this might be a straight racquet while others might have a tilted racquet for top spin or slice.

When you swing your racquet your eyes will never be fast enough to see it but you can see the shadow or silhouette it creates when you swing it and this is what you want to focus on to help you keep your eyes on the point of contact.

- A difficult but fun exercise is having someone feed you some balls while you hit the ball but you will not be allowed to see where it is going. You can only focus on where you hit on the ball. Bottom, top, side or middle is what you want to be able to reply every time you hit the ball. At the beginning it will be hard to resist not watching where the balls lands and if it goes in or out but with practice it will become easier and easier.

# Tip #4: Follow through on all your ground strokes

Under pressure we all shorten our swing thinking it will help make the ball stay inside the lines more often but the exact opposite is true.

Following through is necessary to complete your tennis stroke. Completing a half swing will only give you half as good a shot.

More importantly, repeating the wrong swing (not following through) will only encourage you to do the same in a match situation or under pressure.

Most people follow a similar pattern of shortening their swing more and more the greater their stress level is. In order to change this you want to start making a habit of following through always, on all your ground strokes and serves.

A good drill you can practice to improve your follow through is to mark an "X" on both elbows and then begin hitting some balls. Your practice partner or coach should be able to see the "X" every time you finish your swing and in this way prove you have followed through on your shot. This is a great drill for players who want to improve their follow through in pressure situations.

# Tip #5: Work on serve consistency to win more often

Serving an ace and then a double fault will simply leave you right where you started. Back to even and that's not the goal.

The secret to improving consistency on your serve is to start with a slow speed and gradually work your way to faster speeds as you become more and more consistent.

Being able to reduce the amount of double faults you make in a match can have a serious effect on your match results. Winning an extra game or two versus giving them away in the form of a double fault can mean winning more matches.

**The basic elements to improving serve consistency are:**

- adding some spin to your serve to add control and direction.

- repeating the same motion over and over. Don't try to hit the ball harder and harder and don't change up your serves so often that you can't get a slice or flat serve in because you are varying them too often.

- don't rush. Bounce the ball more often and breathe before serving to help you slow down.
Serving is not a race it's about getting it in as often as possible!

# Tip #6: Return more serves with better footwork

Your feet are connected to your hands and brain. The better your footwork is, the better your hands and brain will react as well.

When you stand at the baseline to return serve it's like starting an engine. That engine needs to get warmed up before going at maximum capacity. The best way to get your body ready to return serve is get your feet moving. Hopping, jumping, alternating leg jumps and jump rope jumps are all good starting points.

The worst thing you can do to return serve is stand flat on your feet so make sure to be on your toes or at least the front of your feet.

Move forward on your return of serve as to turn your body into a moving wall in which the ball will knock into when you hit the ball.

Split stepping and moving around before returning serve is the best thing you can do and will definitely help return more serves no matter how hard or with how much spin they come with.

# Tip #7: Warm up well before the match starts to begin successfully

Getting a jump start on the match makes all the difference in the world and especially in your first set results.

Most people have a very light warm up which includes: stretching, signing with the tournament director or referee, greeting friends, and heading on over to the court to start their match.

**The right way to warm up before your match would be to:**
- do dynamic stretches to get the whole body ready for about 15 minutes (or longer if you feel you need more).

- jog around the court a few times in all directions: forward, sideways, and backwards to loosen up your legs and feet.

- have a light hit with someone you feel comfortable with. Make sure to practice all shots you feel you might be using against your opponent. Basic shots that should always be warmed up are: forehand, backhand, volleys, overhead, and serve. More advanced shots you can warm up and might use are: angled forehands and backhands, drop shots, slice, top spin lobs, etc.

- do a light band warm up if you have been doing bands as part of your warm up but if you have not done bands before, don't start before your match.

- check your bag to make sure you have something to drink, extra grips, towel, extra shirt, extra socks, a healthy snack, etc.

**Tip #8: Stretch after every match to be ready for your next opponent**

After winning your match you will probably have to play your second match within the next 48 hours which means the looser you are, the better you will perform in the matches to follow.

Learn to make it part of your routine, no matter what the results of your match are, to stretch after every match. Sometimes if you win you might decide to celebrate and skip stretching because you won and don't need to stretch. Other times you lose and decide not to even bother with stretching since you lost your match and now it makes no difference as you don't have a next opponent today, tomorrow or all week.

The right way to approach this habit is to understand that getting better at tennis requires ongoing improvement that does not have happen in one day or week. It takes time to slowly develop your game and to do so you have make sure all the pieces of the puzzle are being worked on as often as possible. One of the most important pieces of the puzzle includes your overall mobility which entails becoming more agile and flexible. The best time stretch is when you are very warm and have worked up a sweat. That's why you should do it after your matches.

# Tip #9: Work every point of the match, especially the first points of very game

Do you ever ask yourself what is the most important point of the match? Well it's every point since they're all worth the same. You just have to accumulate enough of them to win the match.

Some points matter more because of the score or the moment in which they are being played.

To get a head start in most tennis matches make it a priority to work extra hard on the first points of every game to begin string in each and every game.

The odds will always be in your favor when you start winning in every first few points of each game and especially after you win the first set. It is said that most people who win the first set win the match 70% of the time which tells you the importance of winning the first set and doing it from the first point on.

A lot of times, starting with a 15-0 or 30-0 advantage in every game gives a mental edge that your opponent cannot deny and he or she will give up many times thinking he or she is far behind in the score. This will be reflected many times with silly unforced errors or way too aggressive points.

Work every point of the match and see how it does wonders for your game and how you will even surprise yourself with wins that you did not expect.

# Tip #10: Close out matches decisively before it's too late

# 12 Tennis Secrets to Win More!

Have trouble winning? Well it might be because you can't do the most necessary of things to win a tennis match. Close it out!

The most difficult thing in a tennis match is many times closing it out. If you can't close a match out, you will never win any matches or tournaments. The truth is, you learn a lot from your losses but you learn to enjoy the game through winning matches.

Winning and closing out matches is important so let's go over some very important things to do when you have the chance to close out a match.

First, figure out what you have been doing to win points in the match as you will probably have a much higher chance at winning match point doing exactly what it took to get you there.

Second, don't let your body freeze. Keep your feet moving and your head up high no matter how tired you are.

Third, stay positive! If your opponent hits an impossible shot and you couldn't do anything about it, don't stress about or get discouraged. How many impossible shots do you think they can hit in a row? Not enough to keep you from winning match point.

Four, learn not to rush on match point. Most errors and bad decisions happen when you rush. Take your time and do things at your own pace even if your opponent complains you are going too slowly.

Lastly, learn to transfer the pressure on to your opponent by bringing them to the net and forcing them to volley or simply pass them. Overheads are highly dreaded shots to hit under pressure as well. You can also rush the net on their weaker side and force them to pass you instead of playing it safe.

# Tip #11: Stay positive no matter what the score or situation of the match

Losing one point, or two or even a whole game is not enough reason to throw the rest of the set or match away due to negativity.

Too often I see the younger players lose important points or a set and then give the next set. This loss of temper or patience needs to be corrected with positive thinking and conviction that they still have a good chance at winning the match.

More and more often professional tennis players are hiring sports psychologists to help them with their mental toughness simply because they understand just how much this aspect of their game can mean to them. Most of the time professional athletes are taught to stay positive under pressure situations. No matter where the pressure comes from.

**Some of the best ways to train yourself to stay positive are:**

- Write down on a stick "stay positive" or "don't give up" or "keep fighting" and stick it on the inside of your racquet where you can see it often. The inside of the neck of the racquet just above the grip is usually the best place. This will remind you what you need to be doing.

- Maintain a positive image of yourself. How you carry yourself will reflect how your opponent sees you and they should see you with: your head up, shoulders back, moving your feet, straight back, etc.

- On change overs put your towel over your head and forget about everything and simply breathe. Once you put the towel back down and stand up reflect the image of a champion as if you have already won the match.

# Tip #12: Use your brain to win more matches and develop your mental toughness

The most important muscle in your body is usually the most under used but it shouldn't have to be that way.

Your brain can be your greatest ally or your worst enemy. Knowing how to use it can benefit every player at every level. Learn to improve your focus, concentration, calmness, thought process, staying positive.

**Try these techniques:**

- Use positive key words like: you can do, keep going, now's your opportunity, get the serve in, just keep running, one more point, and keep your head up.

- Use positive body language to program your brain towards success.

- Keep your mind and eyes on the ball and on your court only.

- Work more on consistency as it is one of the best ways to increase your concentration capacity and focus. Winning one point is good but winning the match requires more than one point.

- Breathe in between points, during points and on change overs. Don't hold your breath as your brain needs oxygen to work and to stay focused.

- Work on visual training to help your eyes stay focused on the ball.

- Practice some pre-match visualization to help you prepare for what you need to be doing on the court later or the next day. For some people this is incredibly powerful so give it a try. Visualize your match and points and shots you want to do in your mind so that your body knows what to do.

The best strategy book around: 32 tennis strategies for today's game

**32 TENNIS STRATEGIES FOR TODAYS GAME**
**By Joseph Correa Pro tennis player and coach.**
Joseph Correa, teaches you the most important tennis strategies around to help you maximize your potential. Learn about: - Basic tennis strategies - Advanced tennis strategies - Mental tennis strategies - and more... Some of the strategies you will learn how to do are: How to beat an all-court player. You can learn: How to beat the "net rusher". How to overcome "lobbers". What to do after you double fault. Learn from the best with this great tennis strategy book that will get you winning more matches and thinking better on and off the court. Win more matches by using the right strategy for each situation. Every player is different in their own way. Some players prefer to stay on the baseline, while others prefer to rush the net. This book will give you the answer to your strategy questions. These 32 strategies will teach you how to beat many different types of players and will help you to overcome mental obstacles through specific mental strategies that are included in this book. For more great tennis videos and books, go to www.tennisvideostore.com

# Bonus: 5 mistakes you probably don't know you're making

# 12 Tennis Secrets to Win More!

## #1 Do ever find yourself looking over at other people's matches?

Start focusing on your own match and not on your surroundings.

## #2 Have you ever found yourself standing around on the court?

Work on keeping your feet moving when you're not on the changeover. This is something very simple to do but highly effective so start doing it.

## #3 Do you give up after you lose the first set?

Most people don't notice just how fast the second set goes by after losing the first set. Don't let losing the first set bring you down. Set your mind on working point by point and game by game not set by set.

## #4 Do you walk right by on the change overs instead of sitting down?

90% of the match is played in your mind so learn to take the time to sit and think things through. Make changes and adjust what needs adjusting until you're playing your best and using the right strategy to win more points.

## #5 You don't need to drink any liquids the night before or the morning of your match?

Where do you think all the sweat comes from when you play the first set? You guessed it! From the liquids you drank at least an hour before the match. Having to go to the bathroom is not a problem but dehydrating is. Drink liquids before and after your match since you don't know if you'll have to play a third set or have to play two matches in one day.

# 15 BONUS SERVE DRILLS TO MASTER CONSISTENCY, SPIN, AND POWER

# 12 Tennis Secrets to Win More!

## 1. Higher First Serve Percentage Drill

Make sure you warm up first before hitting hard serves. First serves can be served flat, with slice, or with kick or topspin depending on what your preferred style of play is so you don't necessarily have to just hit flat and hard. Often players that play on clay use what's called a three quarters serve. This is simply a very fast second serve which is normally done with spin but taking a lot more risk on it.

Start serving on the deuce side of the court. You are going to serve and when the ball lands on the service box you are going to call that "1 first serve in a row". The next serve you hit should go in for you to call it "2 first serves in a row" but if you miss your serve you simply go back to zero. The goal is to get to the highest number of consecutive first serves in. If for any reason you are 10 or 15 serves and miss, you must go back to zero as that is how this drill is done. Once you feel you have reached the highest number possible, you will switch to the ad side of the court and do the same, Switching serving sides is very important since most people serve better off one side than the other but you can only determine this by making sure you give yourself a chance on both sides to determine your highest number possible.

This drill will help you improve your first serve percentages which will normally get more free points in your match. Remember to right done what your highest number was on each side so that you can go back and try to improve off that number the following day or week.

## 2. Higher Second Serve Percentage Drill

The second serve percentage drill is very simple. You're going to start on the deuce side of the court. Begin by serving a second serve and if the serve goes in count "1 second serve in a row". When you get to two serves in a row count "2 second serves in a row". If you miss a serve you must go back to zero. Your goal is to reach the highest number possible as to improve your confidence under pressure and become more consistent.

Once your done serving on the deuce side switch to the ad side of the court and serve from there. Switching is important so that you can figure out on which side you serve better. Most people have a stronger side or a favorite side. Write down your highest number for both sides and then try to improve off that number every time you practice serves.

## 3. Match Preparation Drill

You're going to play a match against yourself and without an opponent on the other side of the court. Begin by serving two serves. A first serve and a second serve. If you get your second serve in you don't have to serve a second serve, just like in a real match. If you get your first serve in you count "15-0" and move on to the ad side as you would normally do in a real tennis match. If you miss your first serve you should serve a second serve. If the serve goes in you would count it as a point but if you miss your second serve you count that point against you as you would normally "0-15". Count just like a normal match. Once you finish the first game, move on to the second game. Your goal is to finish winning the set by reaching 6 games just like a normal match. If you win 6-0 then you should on to the next two drills described below but if you win 6-4 or lose 3-6, you should spend more time on this drill before moving on to the next two drills below.

## 4. Match Preparation Drill for First Serves

You're going to play a match against yourself and without an opponent on the other side of the court. Begin by serving two serves. A first serve and another first serve in replacement of a second serve. If you get your first serve in you don't have to serve a second serve, just like in a real match. If you get your first serve in you count "15-0" and move on to the ad side as you would normally do in a real tennis match. If you miss your first serve you should serve a second serve (which for this drill be another first serve). If the serve goes in you would count it as a point but if you miss your second serve you count that point against you as you would normally "0-15". Count just like a normal match. Once you finish the first game, move on to the second game. Your goal is to finish winning the set by reaching 6 games just like a normal match but by only serving first serves, even when you are supposed to serve a second serve.

This drill will greatly improve your first serve percentage under pressure and in a match.

## 5. Match Preparation Drill for Second Serves

You're going to play a match against yourself and without an opponent on the other side of the court. Begin by serving two serves. A second serve (instead of a first serve) and another second serve. If you get your first serve in you don't have to serve a second serve, just like in a real match. If you get your first serve in you count "15-0" and move on to the ad side as you would normally do in a real tennis match. If you miss your first serve you should serve a second serve (which for this drill be another another serve). If the serve goes in you would count it as a point but if you miss your second serve you count that point against you as you would normally "0-15". Count just like a normal match. Once you finish the first game, move on to the second game. Your goal is to finish winning the set by reaching 6 games just like a normal match but by only serving second serves, even when you are supposed to serve a first serve.

This drill will greatly improve your second serve percentage under pressure and in a match.

## 6. The Side to Side Drill

For this drill you want to start by serving from the deuce side of the court. Start by serving out wide and then switch and serve down the middle or also known as the "center T". Alternate each time you hit a ball so that you never serve to the same side. Once you hit 30-100 balls on the deuce side of the court switch and do the same on the other side. The amount of serves you hit is determined by your level of play and also by how many serves you can hit without hurting your shoulder, especially if you have had shoulder problems in the past.

## 7. The 3-in-1 Serve Drill

For this drill you want to start by serving from the deuce side of the court. You will serve to the three common spots in the service box: out wide, to the body, and down the middle or center "T". Begin by serving out wide first, then make your next serve go to your opponents body, and the last or third ball you serve should go down the middle or center of the court. You're going to repeat the pattern every time to improve your aim.

Once you hit 30-100 balls on the deuce side of the court switch and do the same on the other side. The amount of serves you hit is determined by your level of play and also by how many serves you can hit without hurting your shoulder, especially if you have had shoulder problems in the past.

## 8. The Going Forward Serve Drill

Start by placing a cone about 4-6 feet from the service line in front of where ever you decide to stand when you serve. You will need to serve and then run forward towards the cone and run around it in a counter-clockwise motion and always facing the other side of the court so you never run turning around. When you return back to the service line, take another ball and do it again. The goal is to start making contact more out in front and past the service line as to benefit from being closer to your target which will always be the service box on the opposite side of the court.

This drill will help you do many positive things for your serve:
1. It will improve your toss.
2. It will help you to fully reach forward when making contact so that your arm isn't restricted or tucked in when hitting the ball.
3. The drill will teach you to use your whole body not just your arm to generate power.
4. It will also improve your net game as you will be constantly moving towards the net.
5. You will learn to hit down into the court and not upwards to the other side of the court.
6. Your chin will remain up longer than usual which will get you more balls over the net.

Once you hit 30-100 balls on the deuce side of the court switch and do the same on the other side. The amount of serves you hit is determined by your level of play and also by how many serves you can hit without hurting your shoulder, especially if you have had shoulder problems in the past.

## 9. Serve and Volley Drill

For the serve and volley drill you need to start on the service line. Start by serving and moving forward towards the net. You will need to complete an imaginary volley on the forehand side. I like to call this a simulated volley since you are not going to make contact with any ball on that shot but you will need to use your best technique and effort on it so that you don't just rush through it. The key is to make sure you cross the mid court line before you volley so that you have gone all the way to the net. This is a very physically demanding drill but is worth the effort.

Do this 10-50 times on the deuce side of the court and splitting the serves between half forehand volleys and half backhand volleys when you come into the net. You can add an overhead after the volley which will even further improve your serve and volley game. Total serves would be 30-100 serves on the deuce side. Once you hit 30-100 balls on the deuce side of the court switch and do the same on the other side. The amount of serves you hit is determined by your level of play and also by how many serves you can hit without hurting your shoulder, especially if you have had shoulder problems in the past.

## 10. The Three-Quarters Serve Drill

For the three-quarters serve drill you want to stand on the service line on the deuce side of the court. You will need to serve a fast second serve as to still have some form of control and consistency over the serve but be a lot more aggressive with it. It should be a serve that gives your opponent trouble to return but should not necessarily be an ace. The best way to do this is with a slice or kick serve but can still be done just flat if you don't have any spin serves.

Once you hit 30-100 balls on the deuce side of the court switch and do the same on the other side. The amount of serves you hit is determined by your level of play and also by how many serves you can hit without hurting your shoulder, especially if you have had shoulder problems in the past.

## 11. The "Move Around the Baseline" Serve Drill

For this drill you will need to stand on the deuce side of the service line and start as close to the middle as possible. You will serve from that spot and then take step to the right and serve again. You will repeat this until you get to the doubles alley. At that moment you will begin serving by taking a step to the left as to move back to the middle of the court. Do not rush when doing this drill. Complete a serve and then step to the side and complete the next serve so that you get used to serving from different angles on the baseline.

Once you hit 30-100 balls on the deuce side of the court switch and do the same on the other side. The amount of serves you hit is determined by your level of play and also by how many serves you can hit without feeling fatigued.

## 12. The Variety Serve Drill

For this drill you will need to know how to serve flat, with slice, and with topspin or kick serve in order to perform it. For this drill you will begin by standing on the deuce side of the court and you will start serving a flat serve followed by a slice serve followed by a topspin or kick serve. This order is important but not strict since you can go from a flat serve to a kick serve without a problem and then to a slice serve. The key here is variety. You are not allowed to serve the same serve in a row. You must mix each serve after hitting the last one. This will help you win many more serves and have more service winners because of the difficulty level it will give your opponent. Mixing serves will benefit you more than just being predictable.

Once you hit 30-100 balls on the deuce side of the court switch and do the same on the other side. The amount of serves you hit is determined by your level of play and also by how many serves you can hit without hurting your shoulder, especially if you have had shoulder problems in the past.

Serve flat, slice, top spin serves in that order for 30 balls in a row.

## 13. Power Serve Training Drill

For this drill you want to start by serving from the deuce side of the court. You will begin by serving soft in order to slow bring up the serve speed every time you serve a ball. The first serve you hit should go very slow, the second should go a little faster, etc. When you get to your sixth serve hit , having started soft on serve 1, you should be hitting your hardest. Repeat this process three times going from slow to fast as to warm up you serve and to figure out what you hardest or fastest serve is. Once you know just how hard you can serve you will only serve hard until you hit 20-60 balls on the deuce side of the court switch and do the same on the other side. The amount of serves you hit is determined by your level of play and also by how many serves you can hit without hurting your shoulder, especially if you have had shoulder problems in the past.

Make sure for this drill that you still try to maintain as good technique as possible so that you're now just going for power and losing what's most important for your serve, which is smoothness. Having a smooth and relaxed serve will get you a much faster serve and doing it with proper technique will make it much more possible to do it effectively.

## 14. The Short Court Serve Drill

For this drill you want to start by serving from the deuce side of the court but now you will stand on the mid-court line. Your goal is to serve into the service box as you normally would but now you will be standing much closer inside the court. You are allowed to toss the ball and make contact as out in front of you as you want without foot-faulting. Complete 20 serves from both the deuce and ad sides. Write down how many of your serves landed in and if the second bounce hit the back fence or if it did not reach the back fence. For advanced players, measure just how high on the back fence you hit and work on getting it to reach higher every time. After completing 20 serves on each side while standing right before the mid-court line, take a step back and serve a ball into the service box. Next, take another step back and serve again. Slowly continue taking a step back every time you finish serving until you reach the baseline which is where you will stay once reaching that spot on the court. When you reach the baseline serve 20 more serves from there on both the deuce and ad sides of the court. Once you reach the baseline remember to aim higher on your serve since your serves might tend to go to the net at first because of the angle at which your racquet got used to hitting at when you were at the mid-court line.

## 15. The On-Your-Knees Serve Drill

For this drill you will need a comfortable mat or towel that will not give your knees any pain if you kneel on it. Begin by kneeling on the mat while being right on the baseline on the deuce side of the court. Take a ball and serve into the service box. You will complete a normal serve except the lower half of your body will be eliminated since you will be on your knees. Complete 10-20 serves while on your knees, then stand up and do 10-20 normal serves without the mat. This is your first round of serves. Go back down on your knees and begin the second round of serves. The combination should be a round of serves on your knees followed by a round of normal standing serves. Repeat this process 3 times to complete one side of the court. You should have served 30-60 serves on the deuce side by the time you are done. Once you are done with the deuce side move the mat to the ad side and start the process all over again. By the end of this drill you should have completed 60-120 serves. The amount of serves will depend on you comfort level and just how hard you decide to work that day.

**CAUTION:** Do not complete all the drills above on the same day as you are not supposed to do 1,000 serves in a day or training session. Choose one or two at a maximum for a day or training session and work on those. All of these drill are great and will improve your serve simply choose the ones that you want to do and spread them out during the week or month to get the most out of these 15 drills. Make sure you have someone take a look at your overall technique since that is most important in having a successful serve and will help you reach your potential faster. Stretch and warm up before starting to serve. Jumping rope, jogging, doing ball throws, and doing arm circles are all good ways to warm up before serving.

Good luck in your matches. This book will help you win more matches.

For more great tennis videos and books, check out www.tennisvideostore.com
There you will find titles such as:
Tennis Footwork Training by Joseph Correa
Yoga Tennis by Joseph Correa
The 33 Laws of Tennis by Joseph Correa
Tennis Abs by Joseph Correa
MORE BELOW…

## WOULD YOU DO ME A FAVOR?

Thank you for downloading and reading this book. I hope it was helpful and at least one thing makes you win an extra match or two.

I have a small favor to ask. Would you mind writing a short comment and rate this book on the retail channel you purchased it on?

I like to read all the reviews on my books and enjoy knowing what others think of this book. I feel the best pay comes from good positive reviews from tennis enthusiasts that enjoyed reading it.

If you know of a family member or friend, that you think would benefit from reading this book, please take a minute to share it with them so that they may improve their game as well. I enjoy helping others and would like to answer questions free of charge. You can Tweet me on www.twitter.com at @mybetterswing.com
Check out some of my other books on the next page.

## Other titles by Joseph Correa

### Tennis Serve Harder Training Program

This DVD will teach you how to serve 10-20 mph faster in a 3 month day by day program. The best serve training program in the market. Video includes a 3 month chart training program and a step by step manual. The DVD shows you how to do the exercises properly and the process you should follow in order to be successful with the program.

Joseph Correa is a professional tennis player and coach that has competed and taught all over the world in ITF and ATP tournaments for many years. Besides being a professional tennis player he has a USPTR professional coaching certification and ITF kids coaching certification.

### The 33 Laws of Tennis

The 33 Laws of Tennis is book full of valuable tennis concepts to help you become a better and more prepared tennis player. This book was written by a professional tennis player and coach in the USA. It's a very useful book that will come in handy when you least expect it and will remind you of many little but important things before competing.

### Tennis Footwork and Cardio by Joseph Correa

Joseph Correa is a professional tennis player and coach that has competed and taught all over the world in ITF and ATP tournaments for many years. Besides being a professional tennis player he has a USPTR professional coaching certification and ITF kids coaching certification.

Get in better shape and improve your mobility on and off the tennis court. Your foot work will improve drastically as well as strengthen your core and upper body. This is definitely worthwhile for a serious tennis player no matter what your level. You become faster, stronger, and more agile on the court as well as seeing an increase in acceleration in your groundstrokes and serve. Created by a professional tennis player for others to advance in their game and win more matches.

**Yoga Tennis by Joseph Correa**
Yoga Tennis by Joseph Correa is a great way to improve your flexibility and agility on the court. Reach more balls and have fewer injuries. It's a great way to win more by working on a different part of your game. The DVD lasts about 30 minutes. Used by amateur and professional tennis players to improve their game and last longer in matches. This is the best way for a tennis player to become more flexible and get rid of common back, knee, shoulder, hamstring, calf, and quadriceps injuries. You'll be glad to get started! This is an improved version of our MBS Yoga Tennis 2012.

**The Vilcabamba Diet**
The best diet and exercise book you will find if you want to get in shape and live longer. It's based on a village in Ecuador called "Vilcabamba" where most of its inhabitants live longer than the average person and in great condition. Great for athletes!
Tennis Abs by Joseph Correa
Tennis Abs is a great way to strengthen your core for

more powerful serves, forehands and backhands as well as stronger volleys. Abdominals are fundamental for a better game. This DVD works on many types of crunches, sit-ups, and lateral abs and back exercises that you won´t find in other abdominal videos. Feel confident when changing your shirt during your match and hit the ball harder!

You can find these and other great titles on amazon.com and on tennisvideostore.com

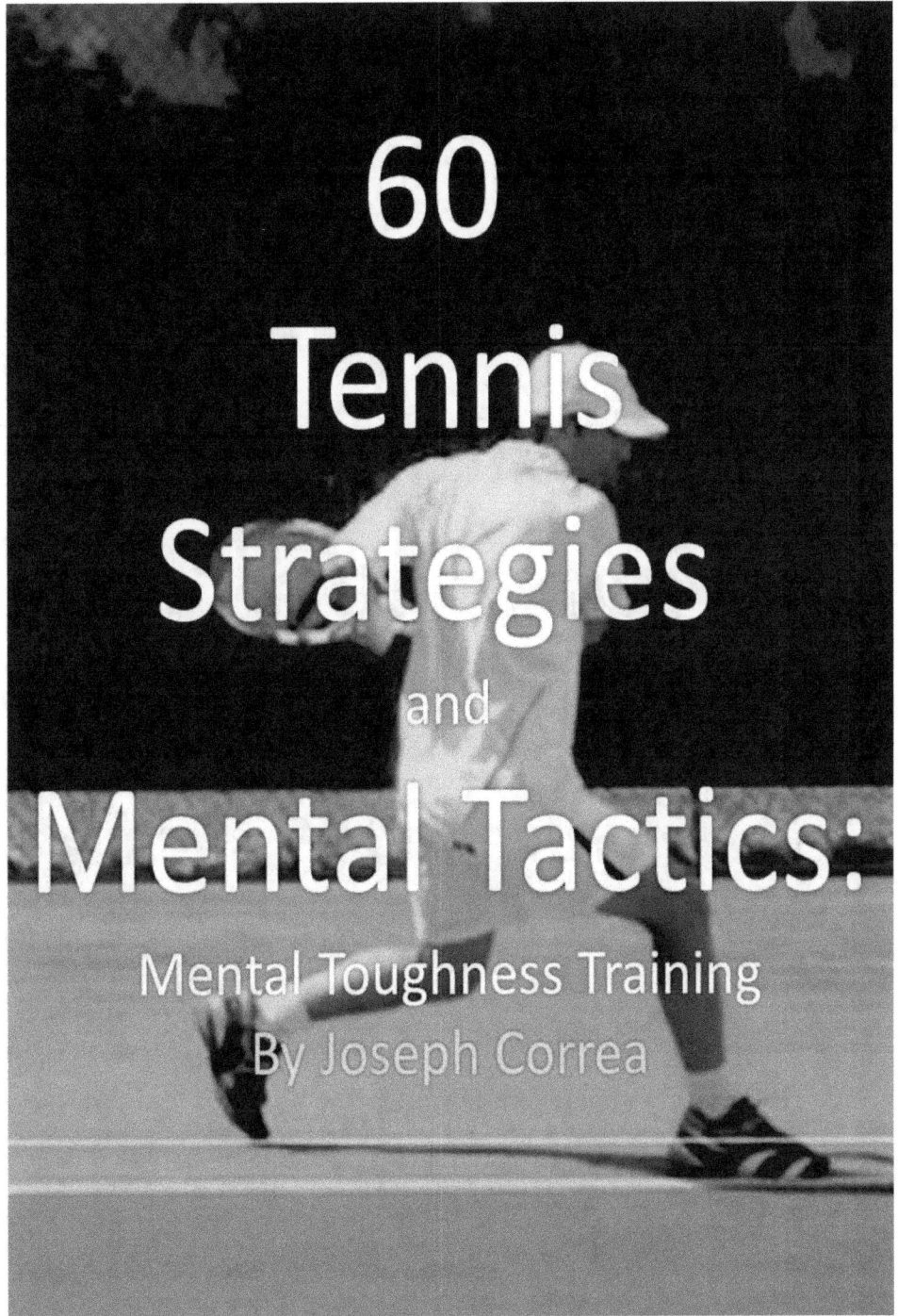

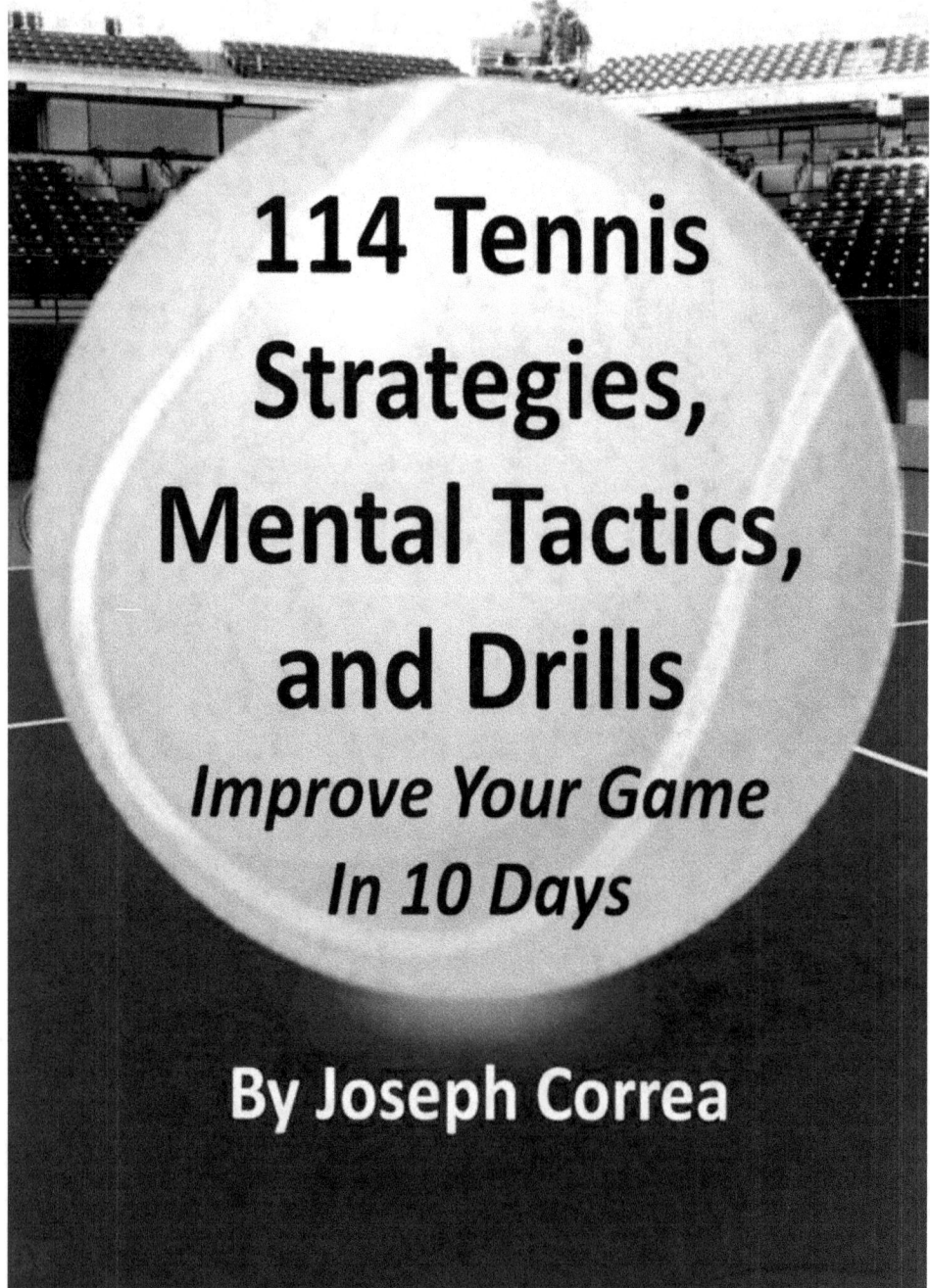

# THE VILCABAMBA DIET

Learn how to live longer and healthier like the people of Vilcabamba!

This book includes:
101 Exercises You Can Do Any Time & Any Place plus BONUS ABS

By
Joseph G. Correa

In Collaboration With
Dr. Juan Carlos Correa

# 12 Tennis Secrets to Win More!

# Superman Tennis Serve

Learn how to serve your fastest serve ever through scientifically proven techniques!

By Joseph Correa

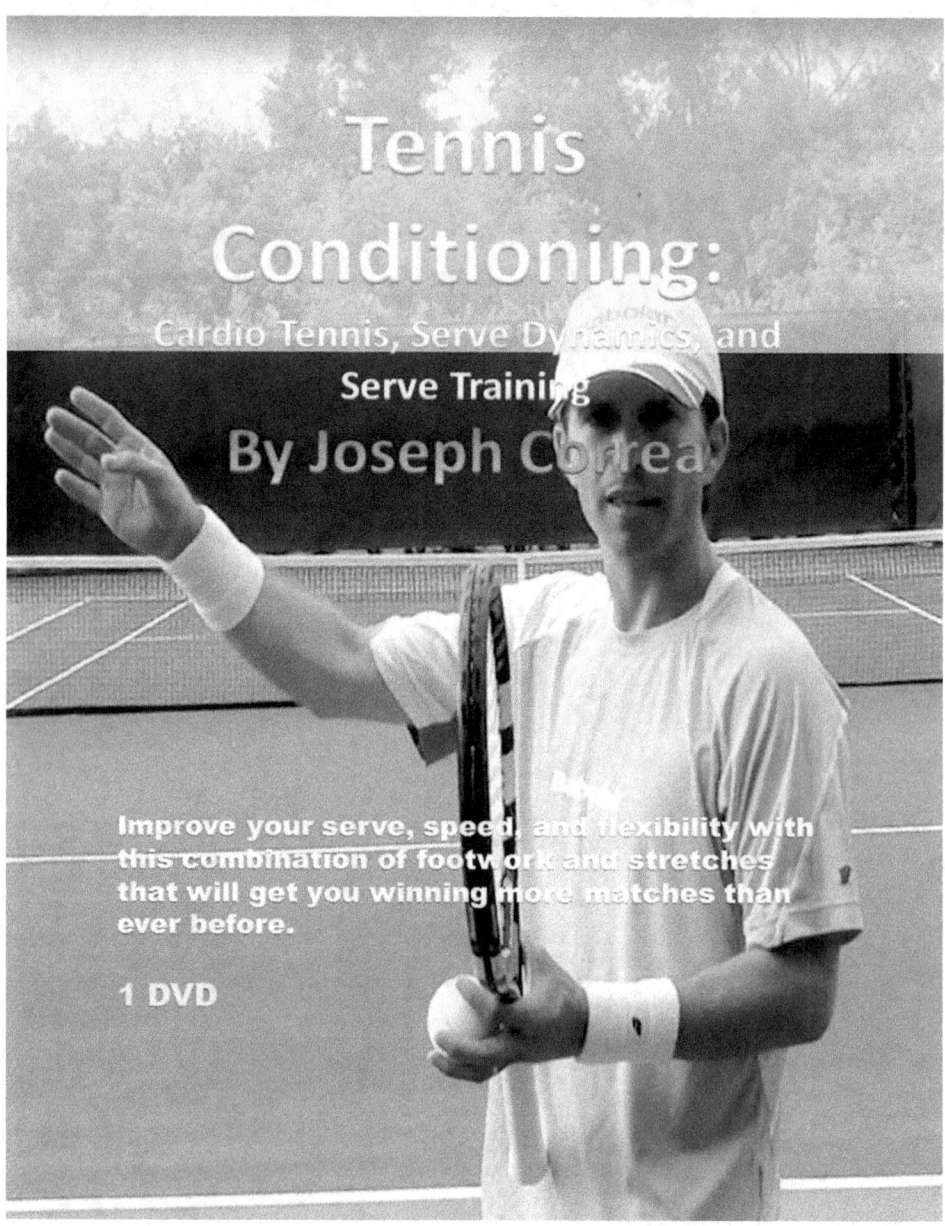

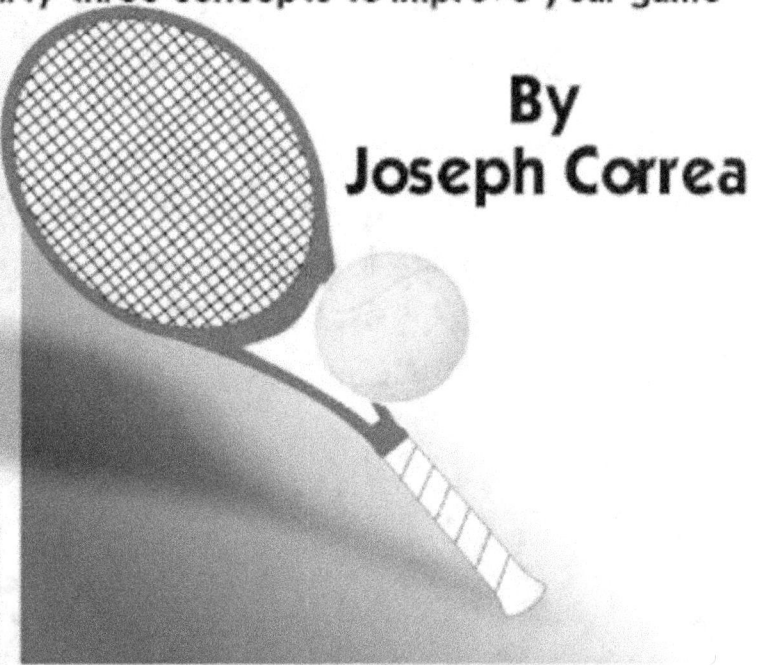

# THE 33 LAWS OF TENNIS

Thirty three concepts to improve your game

### By Joseph Correa

Actual professionals share their trade secrets in this highly practical guide to becoming the best tennis player you can be.

DR. JUAN CARLOS CORREA and JOSEPH CORREA

# The Vilcabamba Diet :

**Lose 10 pounds or more!**

## Lose Weight, Live Longer, and Eat Healthier with the Magic Formula of our Ancestors

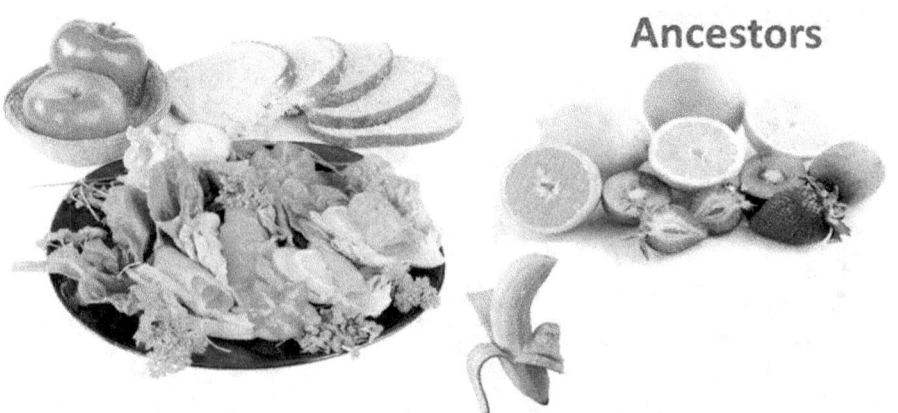

www.ingramcontent.com/pod-product-compliance
Lightning Source LLC
Chambersburg PA
CBHW071215070526
44584CB00019B/3036